C000186876

SLEEPING UNDER THE JUNIPER TREE

Pauline Stainer is a freelance writer and tutor. After many years in rural Essex and then on the Orkney island of Rousay, she now lives at Hadleigh in Suffolk. Her Bloodaxe titles include *The Lady & the Hare: New & Selected Poems* (2003), which draws on five previous books, as well as a new collection, *A Litany of High Waters*; and three later collections, *Crossing the Snowline* (2008), *Tiger Facing the Mist* (2013) and *Sleeping under the Juniper Tree* (2017). Along with *The Lady & the Hare*, her collections *The Honeycomb*, *Sighting the Slave Ship* and *The Ice-Pilot Speaks* were all Poetry Book Society Recommendations. Her fourth collection *The Wound-dresser's Dream* was shortlisted for the Whitbread Poetry Award in 1996. Pauline Stainer received a 2009 Cholmondeley Award for her poetry.

PAULINE STAINER

Sleeping under
the Juniper Tree

BLOODAXE BOOKS

ISBN: 978 1 78037 341 6

First published 2017 by
Bloodaxe Books Ltd,
Eastburn,
South Park,
Hexham,
Northumberland NE46 1BS.

www.bloodaxebooks.com
For further information about Bloodaxe titles
please visit our website or write to
the above address for a catalogue.

Supported using public funding by
**ARTS COUNCIL
ENGLAND**

Cover design: Neil Astley & Pamela Robertson-Pearce.

Printed in Great Britain by Bell & Bain Limited, Glasgow, Scotland, on
acid-free paper sourced from mills with FSC chain of custody certification.

The magnetic beyond looks back

IRIS MURDOCH

ACKNOWLEDGEMENTS

Acknowledgements are due to the editors of the following publications where some of these poems first appeared: *Ploughshares, Poem, Resurgence, Twelve Rivers* and *The Warwick Review.*

CONTENTS

Elijah sleeping under the juniper tree

And it was night.
The angels glowed like phosphors
but gave out no heat.
Beside him, quail
talked of their known world
while he dreamt of paradise-birds
that never alight.

At dawn
he drank of the brook
and ravens came
with bread and delicate meat
until that flower in the wilderness
prophecy
sprang from his throat.

Bach after dark

We are not sleepless
but dream with open eyes
through the Goldberg Variations

the night sky pulses
with the burnished discipline
of fixed stars

each shining turbine
each recapitulation, takes us
beyond bewilderment

Bach improvising on the metaphysics
of radiance, is no music
to sleep through.

Alchemist in search of a voice

Come down, unlikely bird

where there are no inscriptions
in any language

no infrastructure
to quibble with wilderness

no charted interior, save
gossamer between liverworts

no occupied territory, except for
girdled lizard and golden mole

no known reserves, only
unrelated things singing to themselves

the lure of the unsaid
still withholding its miracle.

Nativity with beehives

Seven beehives
the alchemical number of perfection

mother and child
watching worker-bees

hexagons of warm wax
and ancient pollen

honey-wax birds
sipping altar candles

ghostly honey
flicker of souls

setting themselves alight

The marvellous blemish

The past as a raking light,
luminous shards
at the edge of nowhere

shining anguish,
an arrow still fletched
in the glacier

nanocrystals
under the chameleon's skin,
angels with wings of honeycomb

a brocade cloak
at the flagellation,
scarab where the heart was

the gaze of silence
on each bloody meadow,
strata waltzing

such oddities set us adrift
as the dust recollects itself.

Percussion

Once
on these frozen steppes
a nomadic queen
shook out her folded crown
of shivering gold

neutrinos
from that act
without trace
still flash
my closed lids.

Hindsight

That flash as cheetahs
hoodwinked on a leash
are slipped at game

coffins hewn from a single larch
despite the cry
of its original sap

a mummified baby mammoth,
milk in its stomach
still glowing with protein.

At the mind's edge

So many things
apt, inconsequential

flashed ruby
light hinged at the lintel

grave six at the foot
of the night stair.

The muse nothing
if not devious

the heft of an image
outside history.

Pompeii

Here, of all places,
above burnt layer
and bone ash,
a girl, breastfeeding her baby
in a secluded square
beside the forum,
oleanders keeping off the mosquitoes.

And this glimpse –
is it history in the moment
or the moment in history,
mother and child
folded over each other
like doves
drawn with silverpoint?

Burial

Snow fell here once
without wind
on the invisible vole
and the great grey owl
with asymmetric ears.

The control room
(after Eric Ravilious)

Room 29, Home Security,
wartime maps
ghosting the corridor.
Is she typist, telegrapher
or code-breaker, the woman
still at her desk
deep under Whitehall?

Like so many fugitives
she could be unaccounted for
simply pencilled in,
but she sits
unaffected by sunlight
as if soliciting an oracle
in her watercolour grave.

Shaman's mirror

It wasn't the patchwork robe of fur
that fascinated me, so much
as a crystalline disc
clasped to his breast

a masking-agent for the heart,
pencilled in, the way
a silkmoth dissolves
its own cocoon

the green obsidian
in his eye socket
revealing none of those journeys
he made between

inner and outer worlds,
how and where they crossed –
the swift animal,
the nomadic dead.

Water-mirror

We stand in the extreme shallows –
a sheet of *lapis specularis*,
the seeing stone, used like glass

the face of the water
illusionist and threshold,
replay of kingcups

spilling their water-meadow.

The library of water

(after Roni Horn)

A spinney of glass columns
where books once slept,
saplings of meltwater, language illumined.

It sharpens things, altering an element,
as when we made water dance
in a singing bowl

hands beating the meniscus lightly,
memory without mark
written on water.

Closure

Indigo –
that hole in the ice
through which skaters fell
while trees held their sky.

Mark and memory –
the drowned in their
bruising raiment
still stealing the breath.

The glass cloud

Is it bubble or bend in the light?

shimmering out of reach
like mist over a lagoon,
muslin moth, smoking mirror
collision between haze
and disclosure

colour of unknowing
as when gods fling their shawl
over a pillar of cloud
and there is so little dusk
before the night-shining.

Spirit-level

It lies on my desk
made of wood and brass,
air-bubble held in liquid
of supernatural green.
I hold it to the light.

Perfect balance
comes tremulously,
a presage that electrifies,
like that discerning
when imagination answers

the urgency of the image.

Lone Surfer

Master of white inscription,
seven prayers without words
for the seventh wave

the night fathomless,
a running tide, sabres
of watered steel, white jade.

This is the urgency of the body
in its time capsule
while phosphor fish fool past

the flexing indigo
as Odysseus proves the bow-string
to the swallow's indigo answer.

The stilling

(after Leonardo)

And I made
an autopsy of him
in order to ascertain
the cause of so sweet a death

Once you designed machines
to tunnel so silently
dice no longer jumped
on a drumskin

so what did you make
of that simplicity,
the sound
of the heart ceasing?

John Donne arriving in heaven

(after Stanley Spencer)

No phalanx of angels
or field of quintessence –
this is Widbrook Common
near Cookham
with its summer thistles.

No enthusiasm
or shroud of
shockingly vibrant silk,
but a stiff robe, staff
and shadow.

The four praying figures
show no appetite
for any feast of white light.
If the body is a sacred garment
you would never guess it

until you notice how
he leans, leans
into a known landscape
made inexplicably
strange.

Fantasia upon one note

Crucifixion with single angel,
ointment bearers
on a vermilion field,
the heart its own dicebox

and for the feast
of seven sorrows
self-heal, blue-violet,
tender with Paradise.

Lute-maker in a north light

He takes up tiny chisels
like instruments of surgery

physiology of the eye
an intonation in itself

grain of wood and light
grazing one another

bone-lace, inlay
the patience of tranquil alignment

until his sudden impulse
to improvise

that ravishing abstract,
the rose of the lute.

Frankenstein on Orkney

Here,
the lichens are blue-green
like copper silicates,
and everything is horizontal
in the gales that last
for three days.

With this isolation
its a near-certainty
I can cobble together
a second creature
in my new laboratory
beneath the aurora.

I dreamt last night
of an apothecary's rose
where the heart was,
and when I woke
and saw the sun
strike a white-rising lark

I felt such awe and eeriness
I thought of Christ
on Galilee,
summoning, with salt-glazed eye,
the energy with which
to still the tempest.

The jade quarry

They work half-naked
spattered with scars
between runnels of jade

silicates of lime and magnesia,
chemical signatures
adzed away

imperial funeral jades
veined, like the closed
crucible of the heart

glancing accuracy,
such high pressure
in the fissures

none notice brown bears
along the valley
ransacking the beehives.

Japanese acrobats at the Crystal Palace

They tumble past
wearing inflammable fabrics
and smoky colours,
whirling wands with ribbons
of satin and silk

juggling
the sequinned space
between things,
in an intensity of light
like that at high altitude.

For this is the iron and glass house
where huge lily pads glower
from reflecting water,
and as the acrobats build a spangled
pyramid, you wonder

if they lower their heartrate
to sustain such timing.

A step to the Japanese garden

Don't hesitate –
everything is unscripted.
Lotus seeds blow again
after three thousand years.

A wind rakes the gravel
as if marbles are drawn
in silken pouch
across a keyboard.

Nothing awry or ablaze,
lanterns of soulful green,
misty glaze
on driftwood.

Don't expect things
to run ragged.
Only the sparrows
adjourn in uproar.

The bamboo theatre

They have pitched their pavilion
where sleeping lotus
open late in the day

shadow puppets hold the gaze,
until their enchanted interior
is dismantled

and we sense that other gravity,
sap rising, rising
with a waxing moon.

May

It's mesmerising –
the pressure of dust
in light off the saltings
and the way thickets quicken
before there is language
for the leap of a deer
or hares over shingle

The Nine of Hares

(for Lizzie)

Is this how they shed
their seven skins,
coming at things
every which way
in glistening diagonals

or are they celebrating
otherness,
being out of the body,
their mighty haunches
multiplied by the moon
after great dew?

The Copse

I could paint so many happenings –
a slash of chalk,
aspens floating the lake,
foreshore rustling past like silk

successive glazes
on bearded lichens,
disparate weeping of
spindle-berries over water

even at the vanishing point
beyond the copse
there's a release of radiance
like light drum-roll

or the dusky dissolve
of borage fields
over that eternal
underpainting, blue-black

as oilwells burn
for the flight into Egypt.

The brazen foxes

Scavengers, come to haunt the living
where warriors fell between sheaves
of fire and axe.
They burnish the battlefield
with brushes of red-gold.

The dead lie fallow
frost-blue on the furrow.
It's like a deep inbreath
the cunning of colours
in full sunlight.

White doe

End of November,
a ring of peat-coloured cloud
round the moon.
I came upon her in the spinney
strangely unstartled
as if her blood was suspended
whitely in the coming cold.

Everything held a colour not its own.
Furrows ran with quicksilver.
The pallor of her browsing the underbrush
gave me a sense of ceremony,
casual, incarnate
grace
as a mettlesome thing.

Spring snow

We are covered in snowflakes,
shadow-dancers with light-spotted veils,
sugar figures for the dead

so many soundless imprints,
the pressure of snow
on the spoor of creatures.

It's like reading a sacrament.
As Aristotle knew,
even the owls are entranced.

Inner garden

The irrepressible light
is to be dwelt in

as when snow is swept
from a skylight

flakes falling
at different angles

gravitas of wingprint
against glass

a process of otherness
seraphic, slantwise

A place between places

How I longed for it –
an inner isle
at ebbtide

silvered olive groves,
pale dromedaries,
petals brimming a mosaic bowl

the past growing ever lighter
in a freshening wind,
until that bird, the heart

gave its flicker of perfection
before the strangers came.

The anxiety of sunlight

Lightness of being.
Is this it –
detecting ancient fingerprints
in the light?
They outwit us
these lightweight stars,
the last of the light
before there were words
bears no weight of memory.

But this –
the curvature of the earth
bending the sun
into iron-red
while migrating birds
flicker by
like grace-notes
at threshold and source –
This it is.

Borderland

Seven herons
dividing the rushes
to the west of nowhere.

Was it what we saw,
or what we thought we saw?

Eel-grass,
the wind in the reeds
saying the unsayable.

Was it what we heard,
or what we thought we heard?

One thing for certain –
here, the world is hung
on nothing.

The Rosary Quay

Merchant ships ghost by
deep-laden as the estuary
silts up

where sailors slept
in hammocks, children skate
between the wharves

the rhythm of cargoes
hangs like heavy dew
from the hawsers.

Above the canal
artisans carve rosaries
for lace-maker and tallow chandler

and a nun
in a white coif
still trims the candles

as if for a moment
the known world is
diminuendo

The invisible year

It was the year
I saw a white swallow
against the white night

everything attuned to erasure,
glass-fish, silver-lined
pearled, perishable

the island unfrequented,
no blessing of ashen vessels
as the moon altered the sea

leaves under ice
sheer twice over
like a half-tone tattoo

pure *solutio*
of alchemy,
the last magician.

The convention

Magicians once gathered
in the Winter Garden

behind boarded windows
their wizardry still flickers

sleight of hand
white dove after white dove

the endless arterial red
conjured from a breast pocket

Snowfall in Babylon

Not sandstorm
but snow so thick
one creature might metamorphose
into another

carnivores,
small Babylonian lions
slink like quicksilver
under the hanging gardens

where harps hung
from the willows,
the recurring slash
of history

is snowed under,
perfect camouflage
white on red
red on white

as each breast is opened
and lilies spill out.

Forest with mistletoe

We would never have guessed
that once the moon rose here
like a copper vessel,
as prisoners in rope-soled shoes
soaked up blood dark as mulberry juice

but suddenly, we saw bundles
of gauze in the high branches,
the golden parasite
shivering with myth,
soft overspill of massacre.

Resource

There's nothing like listening
to unseen birds in the reeds

invisibility
assuaging the water

while downriver
as in an Egyptian tomb

the eye of a hunting cat
is gilded.

Rewilding

Beyond and backlit –
oil tankers
in their molten silks.

Give us the sweet pressure
of pasture, its deed of variation
where herds suckle and graze.

Let them not falter,
those fields flexing with beasts
on their blue way through.

Avoriaz

That June
walking under balsam poplars,
I remembered Avoriaz

the way a cube of mist
was held momentarily
between ski-slopes

crazy apartments
clad with cedar shingles
lilting through sleet.

It still disorientates,
such vibrancy of absence,
frost falling after dark

over pastures withholding
their sweetness.

Aftermath

After the mowing
we lay down in the meadow,
our bodies figured silk

everywhere,
residues of ancestral pollen,
chemical transfer between cells

our single imprint on the aftermath
the naked ground
of being.

After Gerhard Richter

Each blur
is a field of energy,
as when the dew-eagle
with pool of dew upon his back
lets spill
a mist-net for singing birds.

Against this, I lay that surgery
which seals a wound
as it is made,
the god eliciting
one of Adam's ribs
and closing up the flesh
instead thereof,
as with a diathermy blade.

The shape of forgetting

Is it burn or bleach-out,
the portal
between eclipses

John Clare dreaming
of Mary lying
on his left arm

even though she will
never watch for the morning?

The Mondaytown bat

(for Juliet)

Deep twilight,
the purple tincture
of Renaissance painters,
familiar flicker
of a single bat
round the eaves
as night falls

dawn,
swift dispensing of mist
into ash-blue.
We found its tiny corpse
on the grass,
no visible wound,
just inimitably mortal.

Accidentals

The quicksands are profoundly silent

only the frisson
of a small amulet
in the wound

Roman nails with magic symbols,
a helmet with
slightly parted lips

slaves, gold and salt –
the ice closes
behind each sterilised probe

Let them lie a little remote
and like migrating birds
grow lighter

The leavening

Nuns have brought
kneaded dough into the chapel
where it rises without a draught

silence brims
with this creature of bread,
the smell of yeast against stone

while outside,
the perfect accident
of corn ripening the light.

Afterlife

Things grow foreign at dusk –
gravestones in the form of sheep,
Siberian nomads
with boots of silver fox fur
a wolf's foot on the lintel

astrologers, physicians, falconers,
emperors of the afterlife,
their animals still groomed
for sacrifice
in the apricot orchard

and *sotto voce*, the frisson of their dust –
Have done, have done,
only the fool
surprised by light
gets by.

Prophecy

The sky was scowling purple
streaked with vein-blue
when a merlin
smallest of falcons
flew past so low and close
its subtle body
touched me a moment
inside the mouth.